W9-ABW-986

Shoes
in
VOGUE

Shoes in VOGUE

SINCE 1910

by Christina Probert

ABBEVILLE PRESS · PUBLISHERS · NEW YORK

ACKNOWLEDGMENTS

So many people have shared their talents with *Vogue* over the years: artists, photographers, designers, craftsmen, writers, but also *Vogue*'s own editors whose perspicacious choices have shaped the magazine. I am grateful to Mandy Clapperton, Edward Rayne, Roger Bromley, Richard Smith, Mandy Wilkins and James Boswell who generously shared their knowledge of the shoe trade with me. I am indebted to Alex Kroll, Editor of Condé Nast Books, for his guidance throughout, Georgina Boosey for her editorial wisdom, Liz Bauwens for the book's design, Trudy Lee for her advice and ever-present help.

C.P.

© 1981 by The Condé Nast Publications Ltd.
First published in the USA in 1981 by Abbeville Press, Inc.

Library of Congress catalog card number 81-67880

ISBN 0–89659–241–3

Cover. BV 1978 Albert Watson. *Manolo Blahnik (left), Ivory (right)*. Back cover. FV 1923. *Hellstern*
Page 2. BV 1975 Keith Collie. *Russell & Bromley*

CONTENTS

Key to captions

Information is given in the following order: edition; year; artist or photographer;
designer or maker (the last always in *italic*). Editions are identified by initials:

AV   American *Vogue*
BV   British *Vogue*
FV   French *Vogue*
IV   Italian *Vogue*
GV   German *Vogue*

INTRODUCTION

'Her feet beneath her petticoat
Like little mice, stole in and out
As if they feared the light.'

Sir John Suckling (1609–42).

True beauty traditionally requires tiny, delicately formed feet. Suckling's heroine had feet like 'little mice', while Cinderella's, the most famous of popular fable, were the tiniest in the land, her sable slipper so small it fitted no other girl. The bound feet and tiny shoes of Chinese women were as much a mark of class as of fashion or beauty. In eighteenth century England and France foot size was seen as a mark of social standing: portrait sitters were always given tiny feet, for large feet were a sign of low birth. During the early years of the twentieth century this idea gradually lost favour, and by 1930 society women were dashing down ski slopes, playing tennis, gardening, and wearing for all of these, wide soft footwear which allowed the feet to spread.

Fashion and etiquette have not always permitted exposure of the shoe-makers' craft: for Suckling, in the seventeenth century, a fleeting glimpse of a foot was exciting. The fashions of the late eighteenth and early nineteenth centuries made such a glimpse commonplace, but with Victoria's accession (her sartorial influence was international) came darkness for the feet, hidden under swathes of petticoat, crinoline, skirts until the twentieth century.

By 1880 women began to indicate that they were capable of more active occupations than those permitted by popular attitudes and restricting clothes. The 'Rational Dress' movement, for example, advocated styles based on considerations of 'health, comfort and beauty'. Such sentiments had become widespread by the early twentieth century. The Great War formalised the sea change taking place. Women wore practical clothes and shoes to do vital, practical jobs: those who drove ambulances for the first time, dressed wounds and clothed refugees, there could be no going back to a world where they were considered incapable of lifting a tea-tray. Women's suffrage movements were achieving their goal by 1920; women's athletics established themselves; women took full or part-time jobs: and all these new aspects of life naturally affected what women wore.

In 1910, walking boots were essential outdoor wear, winter and summer; shoes were high-cut, supportive, and only in the boudoir were hemlines ankle-length, shoes delicate and soft. Footwear fulfilled the same function for the feet that corsets did for the body: indeed restricting footwear and corsets ceased to be *de rigueur* simultaneously in the early 1920's as a result of

Cinderella's 'glass' slipper recreated as 1973 fashion in Perspex and speckled leather, and painted for British *Vogue*. BV 1973 Michael English. *Richard Smith*

1910

'*La chaussure de Cendrillon*': Cinderella's shoe in the current mode. FV 1919 George Barbier

The Louis heel: high cut evening shoe with beaded tulle bow. AV 1911. *Frank Bros.*

The draped, bifurcated skirt, considered shockingly revealing: the ankles and shoes were on show! AV 1911

women's new role. At the outset of the century weather, season, time of day, rather than personal choice, dictated the style and even colour of shoes. Interest in shoes tended thus to focus on good cut and high quality, which were far more keenly sought after than they are today. A Fifth Avenue shoe shop, for example, advertised some evening slippers in 1919 captioned: 'In these, as in our shoes for women and men, superiority is manifest. They have that indescribable touch of smartness that commends them to people who are particular.'

Editorial remarks on footwear were scarce in the first eighteen years of the century. An early shoe editorial which appeared in February 1911, entitled 'The well shod foot: Good style boots and slippers and some little accessories that save hosiery wear', was as matter-of-fact as a train timetable, and the advice included as constant. As *Vogue* was to remark in 1919: 'At the beginning of the War we were limited to the prescribed boot for walking . . . now our choice of shoes has become more unlimited than ever, and the subject of footwear fascinating enough to talk about at length.'

The ubiquitous Victorian buttoned or laced boots remained correct out-door wear until 1920, when they were relegated to footwear for the elderly and infirm. By 1910, however, it became increasingly acceptable to wear lace-up shoes or 'ties' as an alternative to boots, now ankle-length, in fine weather. In winter, boots and shoes were made of leather and suede; later versions in toning shades of browns in addition to the plain brown and black worn throughout. In summer, white suede or buckskin, beige and mush-room suede leather were correct. Heels varied in height between 2 inches and $2\frac{1}{2}$ inches and in shape from the Louis in 1900 to the Cuban. Louis heels, named after Louis XIV, were waisted all round, giving a splayed out effect at its base, the shape Cinderella's Ugly Sisters still often wear in English pantomime. The Cuban heel, shaped only at the back, reappeared spasmodically throughout the twentieth century.

For daytime in 1910 indoor shoes were pumps, again with little $2-2\frac{1}{2}$-inch heels, made of glacé leather or kid, in black or tan and only lightly ornamented with self-coloured pom-pons or bows. By 1914, the variety of colours and fabrics had become much greater as the rules of etiquette softened: decoration became increasingly important, varying from season to season.

Evening and boudoir shoes were always the least closely regimented and thus their styling was the most open to interpretation. Bedroom slippers in 1910 were flat or Louis-heeled, of suede, kid, velvet, lace, satin or brocade, ornamented with bows, ties, frills, buckles, pom-pons and ribbons. Drawings of exotic and fashionable bedroom slippers in early July 1919 were captioned by *Vogue*: 'The world is proved an ensnaring place when slippers and mules for slender bare feet droop their delicate frills or flaunt their bright ribbons with unmistakeable coquetry.'

High cut evening shoes, a necessity in 1900, were worn until the second decade of the century, when strapped and laced versions became alternatives. These were much less highly cut over the instep, thus giving greater flexibility for dancing. By 1911 an editorial admitted that 'one is granted great leeway in these shoes' and illustrated a pair of high-cut black satin shoes with a butterfly bow of beaded black tulle. Whether of kid, velvet or suede, black evening shoes were correct wear until after the Great War, illustrated in *Vogue* in fashion sittings and photographic portraits. Even during the war greater leeway was allowed in styles, and coloured evening shoes appeared, dyed to match a ball dress, for example. Skirts shortened at the end of the war and there was a sudden surge of interest in what was on the feet. In 1919, Baron De Meyer, then under contract to *Vogue*, photographed walking, house, wedding and evening shoes for *Vogue*'s first sizeable photographic shoe article 'New shoes for Cinderella'.

Shoe decoration was particularly interesting in this early period. The earliest types were bows and pom-pons of satin or tulle or even of kid, sometimes beaded or ornamented with silver tissue (fine silvery chiffon). Most ornamentation was focused on evening and bedroom shoes and mules, but some walking and house shoes were also buckled and laced, even in 1910. The shape of buckle which first became fashionable was large and square; it gradually became smaller and, later still, round, oval, butterfly or bow-shaped. Early versions were made of burnished steel, later of paste, facetted cut steel or steel set with seed pearls. By 1920 feathers, rosettes, fur, velvet ribbons, lace and embroidery were all being used to decorate shoes that now 'deliberately ask attention'.

Legs, too, had become more brightly clad: silk stockings were finer, colours more varied and the necessary seaming transmuted into decorative patterns. Lisle stockings were worn throughout both decades for active sports, walking and general daytime wear. Although coarser and less fitting than their silk counterparts, they were far less expensive and harder wearing.

'A woman has a natural weakness where hosiery is concerned. Silk stockings are certainly seductive and cannot be withstood', said *Vogue* in 1911, and proceeded to list a variety of types of silk stocking; ribbed, plain-knit, two-tone and cotton-footed, calculated to ensure that the weakness would not be withstood. In 1919, Chantilly lace inserts in white silk stockings were particularly fashionable for evening; embroidered inserts were unusual for daytime wear.

By 1920, shoes had become a fashion accessory as important as a hat had always been, or gloves, or a handbag. Indeed, now that shoes were so attractive, so bright and so much on display, one had to be 'more careful than ever to place one's feet prettily, for the most charming footgear in the world will not better an unattractive walk'.

White lace stockings for the newly visible ankles. B V 1919 De Meyer

Pyrographed shoes 'for the boudoir of the deliciously impractical Parisienne'. B V 1919 George Barbier

1920

AV 1909

BV 1918. *Swan & Edgar*

The first editorial shoe pictures to appear on *Vogue*'s pages, *opposite*. Interest in shoe design and colouring increased as hemlines shortened: decorative stockings like these *on the right* emphasized this newly visible zone. By 1910 the new Cuban heel was used for walking and some evening styles, *opposite below left and right*; but for **evening** and boudoir shoes, like the **lace-up** and stripy versions *above*, the Louis heel remained the **most** popular almost until 1920. Swan & Edgar's advertisement of 1918 shows how little the shape of shoes had **changed** since 1910; what had changed **was** their fabric and finish: buckles and bows, new **details** each season – brocade, quilted **satin**, velvets used for late day and **evening** shoes, suedes, silk, glacé and plain leathers too.

A V 1910 Transatlantic Company

An expanse of leg clad in newly sheer silk stockings on show as hemlines rise towards 1920. There had for some years been dispute between Parisiennes and Englishwomen over the rectitude of the English last, long and narrow with a pointed toe, or the French last, wider and less pointed. The shoes *above* and boots and sandals *below* show the *Entente* reached by 1920: a more rounded toe, width of shoe midway between the traditional English and French lasts, heels the international Louis shape. More instantly recognizable changes were taking place too – the shoes *opposite*, of flesh-coloured satin with satin fans behind tiny buckles, were high fashion in 1919. Only a year later appeared the black velvet slippers *above*, appliquéd with geometric designs in white grosgrain ribbon, an early indication of fashion's new mood in the twenties.

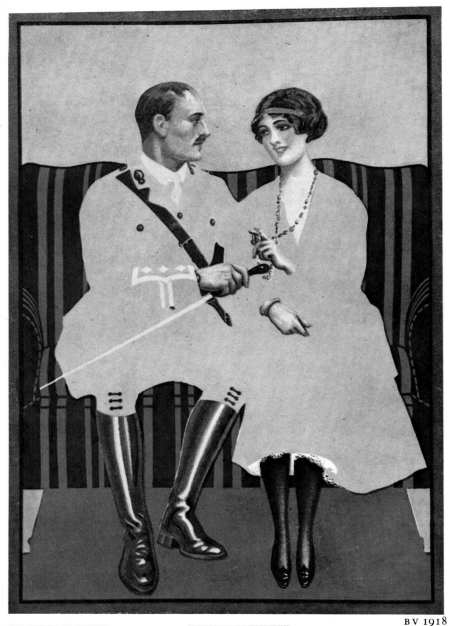

BV 1918

AV 1913

AV 1911

The whole range of garb for the well-shod foot, 1911–19. *Left* are two pairs of boots: punched leather pointed and laced boots for walking and a higher cut, simpler version for riding. Simplest of all, *above right*, polo boots of firm leather, similar to the cavalry boots in the adjoining picture. Discretion characterized fashionable footwear: the lady, *above*, in afternoon dress, wears simple pointed pumps, the uppers subtly decorated, and the evening slippers, *left*, are of dark velvet with a 'fancy buckle'. Boudoir shoes are the exception: multi-coloured laces, velvets, silks were used, and the languid lady *opposite* wears green slippers, with little white pompons.

BV 1919 George Plank

Shoes in the spotlights, *opposite*. Jane Renouardt, *far right*, in *Moune* at the Variétés in Paris, wears a Callot gown in cream tulle, silver embroidered lace and gold tissue. Her shoes of cream satin have Louis heels, pointed toes, small buckles. The Louis heel ruled the New York stage too: the heroine of *The Lassoo* wears similar shoes, *right*, laced around the ankle, with her Lucile dress of Valenciennes lace and hydrangea chiffon. Norma Talmadge's, *opposite below left*, are a more pointed version worn with a 'costume as clever as her acting'. Out on the street, however, boots are still fashionable: these black patent and grey kid boots, *this page*, which button at the side are still correct wear, particularly in inclement weather.

BV 1917

BV 1918

BV 1917

17

1920

The twenties produced some of the most exciting shoes of the century, a tremendous variety of cut, colour and ornamentation influenced by the period of Louis XIV and by the Italian Renaissance. 'There is a noticeable tendency', said *Vogue* in 1921, 'to get away from shades which merely match the costume and to introduce a note of decided contrast.' All eyes were thus focused on the feet, newly arched on high heels, clad in bright, rich fabrics and colours: silver and gold brocade, velvets, silks, embroidered fabrics, beadwork and sequins. This riot of colour and texture was a result not of gradual change in fashion, but of a complete break with tradition.

During the 1914–18 war, both functional and fashionable clothing had hidden the legs and feet, the latter clad in sombre colours. Some restrictions on 'frivolous' dress had been necessitated by the demands of war work on the labour forces. Yet these restrictions were far less stringent than they were to be in the next war: French fashions still appeared in Britain and the United States. The most forceful limitation was that of public opinion; it was *a la mode* to appear to engross oneself in the war effort rather than spend time considering one's latest pair of shoes.

Now, in the twenties, there was a new sense of freedom in dress. Undergarments were softer and looser, hemlines rose fast towards the knee, showing a new length of leg. Naturally, shoes and stockings became focal points of fashion. Suddenly everyone wanted short skirts, everyone wanted coloured stockings, and everyone wanted new shoes. Fashions changed radically from season to season, and there could be no question of wearing one season's shoes for a second. At the outset of the decade the readymade shoe industry had not made much headway into the fashion market. The sudden increase in demand stimulated expansion, and many new shoe companies and shops were established; made-to-measure shoemakers could not keep pace. Editorials of the twenties show the tremendous variety of styles, the increasing number of manufacturers and retailers, and testify, too, to the surge of excitement and new ideas in shoe design.

The twenties shoe was high-heeled, even for dancing. At the outset of the decade heels were curvy, in Louis XIV style. The squatter and lower Cuban heel came into fashion for sports and walking shoes in 1922, and this straighter shape influenced the high heels worn for dancing and daytime later in the century. The pointed shoe with high heel and single bar strap over the instep is traditionally considered to be the twenties shoe, and is indeed the strongest shape of the decade. Other shapes were important too: tongues in 1922, cutaways in 1923, T-bars and crossover straps in 1924. The court shoe (a debased version of the traditional tied patent court presentation shoe) continued to be an important shape. After 1926 the shoe's silhouette

For sports: topstitched chestnut leather shoes worn with Scotch wool stockings. F V 1923

For the afternoon in the early twenties: satin slippers with buckles of brilliants, lace stockings. B V 1920 De Meyer

The new higher, less curved heel for daywear. A V 1922 Nickolas Muray. *Henning*

became lighter, straps narrower, shaping more delicate as a calmer atmosphere penetrated the fashion world after the fervid activity of the preceding few years.

The almost infinite variety of colours, and mixes of colours and fabrics, used in the early twenties are still exciting to see, even after sixty years. Hellstern (perhaps the most fashionable shoemaker, internationally, of the decade) was using such exotic fabrics as silks embroidered all over with pearls, gold lamé, colour mixes like red and white, red and blue leather; he made great use of coloured and carved heels, and of appliqué leather. The influence of the Orient and of Greek art was particularly strong in the early twenties, producing pyrographed shoes (a kind of embossed leather process, often depicting Greek vase scenes) and richly coloured and embroidered 'harem' slippers and mules.

As with shape, after the middle of the decade colour mixes became subtler as the shoe became once again an accessory and no longer the focal point. Browns, greys and greige became fashionable; correspondingly, bright colours began to be used in less startling combinations, the two-tone sports shoe became tones of brown rather than black and white. Appliqué leather was often patent appliquéd onto suede or kid in a similar colour. Gold kid, in fashion since 1922, was superseded by argenté kid in the last three years of the decade. Kid was often used as cutwork superimposed on velvet, silk or leather, also as straps (which became narrower and narrower) and as a heel covering in a contrasting colour. Art Deco shoes in bright colour mixes like brown and yellow were fashionable still in 1926, the aftermath of the Exhibition of Decorative Arts in 1925, in Paris; but subtler effects, like woven straw, pearlized leather, crepe de chine and kid, were more generally popular as 1930 approached.

Buckles were by no means addenda in this decade. Already ornate in 1920, after passing through many forms during the early part of the century, the buckle now became important more for its substance than for its shape. Pearls and diamanté were popular initially; bronze buckles appeared in 1922 and mirror sequins in 1924, in accord with Eastern fashion in clothing. Then 1925 brought mother of pearl and silver enamelled with primary colours, and in 1926 buckles were loaded with 'precious' stones, diamanté and onyx. As shoes became lighter, straps finer, the size of the buckle decreased and by the end of the decade had become small, functional and neat for day wear, of decorative importance only on evening shoes. As French *Vogue* said in 1930: 'the only applied ornament which is now *bon ton* is that which is almost imperceptible'.

For evening, sandals were important throughout the decade these in brocade, bound with matching metal cloth. A V 1922 Nickolas Muray. *Henning*

1930

FV 1925 Benito. *Greco*

BV 1924. *Jacobus*

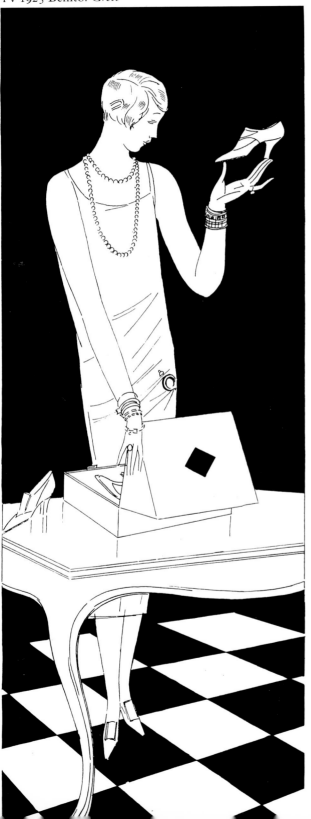

FV 1926 Abbé

By 1925 hairstyles were boyish, as short as the newest dresses of silk, chiffon, silvered, beaded and embroidered fabrics. The feet and legs, increasingly on show, became focal points. Colours and fabrics were bright and daring, particularly for dancing shoes like these *opposite above and below right*: red, yellow and gold zig-zag brocade on high heels to Charleston in, *above*; black and white cutwork ankle-strap shoes worn by Spirelly, *below*, in Alfred Savoir's *L'Anglais tel qu'on le mange*. The choice of styles was great throughout the twenties: Pandora, *opposite left*, ponders over the possibilities in her box, while her less fortunate counterpart, *this page*, imagines the shoe wardrobe of her dreams. Clockwise *from bottom left* are evening shoes: black, rose and silver brocade on silver heel, silver tissue with one strap over the instep, black satin with a gold heel and embroidered border. For the boudoir: red kid mules lined with white, bright leather heeled slippers with fur edging. Daytime shoes: triple-barred stamped silk and gold kid shoe, black satin high shoe embroidered with pearls, satin shoe with double strap and buckles with brilliants.

BV 1927. *Left: London Shoe Company, Rayne, Manfield, Rayne. Right: all Greco*

Left, 1925: the simplest silver kid shoes for dancing, very high, very elegant, worn with tiered beaded dress and huge earrings reaching down to this flapper's beaded and sashed neck. The lady *opposite* shows us her tiny Christmas package, on display in a deep green suede shoe: the separated back and V-shaped pointed front are both fashion points of 1924. The curvy heel, high fashion in 1919, had by now disappeared from the scene: both the green and silver shoes have straight heels.

BV 1925 Meserole   FV 1924 Lepa

V 1928 Steichen. *Slater*

Colour, texture and sparkle: fabrics and finishes of
the twenties. Buckle designs, which had changed
faster than shoe shapes early in the century,
remained lively when shoe design accelerated in the
twenties. The black satin pump, *opposite*, has a
crystal buckle similar to Chanel's jewellery launched
in the twenties. On the cushion, *below*, are four oval
1916 buckles, of brilliants and pearls.
Six diverse Art Deco designs of 1926 on the
buckle tree: enamel, mother-of-pearl, diamond and
silver, onyx set in agate and diamond. New and
exotic shoe fabric textures in 1927: the blue and
white straw shoe *right* has blue kid trimming, the
two *below* are pearlized kid, with black and
metallic brocade on gold, silver mesh on mauve
pearl kid.

A V 1927 Steichen. *Henning*

A V 1927 Steichen. *Vida Moore*

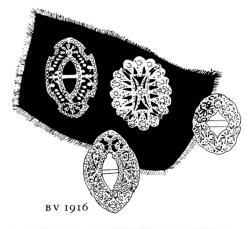

B V 1916

B V 1926

Subtler colour combinations for both day and evening as the twenties progress. Daytime shoes, *this page*, in shades of brown from rust to copper and cocoa for the Oxfords of cordovan leather, walking brogues of willow calf, *left. Next and top right* are for town walking, the court fashionably high cut, of gunmetal leather, the other two of punched calf; (5), (6) and (7), smart afternoon shoes, have lizardskin details in modernistic style and the new narrow straps. The evening shoes on the steps and fan, *opposite*, demonstrate the wide choice of styles and finishes in the late twenties. *From left to right* on the fan: two shoes with piped silver detailing; a basket-woven leather court shoe; gold and silver jazzy strapped, low cut shoe; red satin plain court with intertwined straps over the instep; leather and snakeskin ankle-strap shoe. On the bottom four steps, *opposite right*, are evening shoes in bright satins with gold and silver kid cutwork, lots of fine straps. *Above* them are two brocade shoes, pink and gold, a pyrographed gold leather shoe and a very cutaway Art Deco sandal. Daytime and evening shoes 1929-style, around the 'moon' opposite, have still higher heels, narrower too, clean lines and little ornament.

DAYTIME SHOES

BV 1927. *From left: Harvey Nichols, Norvic, Rayne, Hanan, Jacobus, Excelsior, Lilley & Skinner, London Shoe Company*

F V 1926 Libis. *Perugia*

B V 1929 *Clockwise from top right: Lilley & Skinner, London Shoe Company, Manfield (2), London Shoe Company, Hanan (2), Lilley & Skinner*

B V 1927 J. Pagès. *From bottom: Ducerf Scavini, (1) and (2) Greco, (3), (7) and (8) Hellstern, (4), (5) and (6)*

27

1930

New shaped heel for a new decade. This tailored, practical shoe is the look of the thirties. FV 1935. *Bentivegna*

Sport becomes a fashionable preoccupation: Princesse Cyrille Troubetzkoi in the latest golf shoes with rouleau ties. FV 1938. Schall

The rules of etiquette which governed dress had relaxed during the twenties. Fashion had become noticeably less formal, and the borderlines between types of shoe had blurred. With the thirties shoes became tailored again to the various parts of the day's routine: 'To have shoes on one's feet is now more nearly described as to be wearing the kind of shoes dictated by time of day and circumstances. The nuances between active sport shoes, walking shoes, stroll-in-the-park shoes and smart afternoon shoes are clearly visible,' said French *Vogue* in 1936. New, widespread interest in active sports created further species of shoe: for golf, sailing, shooting, tennis. New, too, were trousers as casual wear; the silhouette of the trousered leg demanded special shoe styles, as did the longer lengths of evening gowns, suits and dresses. The look of the decade was 'classic': elegant, calmer, more sinuous than that of the twenties, the very best of cut, fabric and finish.

Comfort was now a major consideration in the fashion world: *Vogue* ran a feature, in 1935, on shoes chosen by various personalities, all of whom laid great emphasis on the necessity for wider, soft shoes as opposed to the long, slim, rather rigid shapes of the twenties. Shapes did become broader and toes less pointed, a result both of this healthy attitude towards comfort, and equally of the newly fashionable suit. This more tailored style demanded a more imposing shoe.

The newer heel was lower, solid, while still curved rather than angular, with a wider base. This shape stayed in fashion until the end of the decade: the high heel of the twenties remained for evening shoes, but gradually lost its pre-eminence. There were many new and interesting shapes: in 1937 clog soles, the following year the platform sole, unforgettably clad in sequins, embroidery and bows for evening. Both this sole and the wedge which followed it continued to be in fashion for some time: they had all the advantages of comfort and practicality. The Cuban heel was the smart sports heel, but after 1934 completely flat sandals and sports shoes became popular with shorts and trousers.

The cut of clothes in the thirties was of paramount importance, the line svelte and fitting, whether in evening dress, suit or sailing outfit. Likewise the matching shoes: not always plain, they were less cluttered than the twenties shoe and built on clean-cut lines. The shape was higher cut, the front covered the upper instep as the decade progressed, lacing came back into fashion, and the higher cut look extended even to sandals which had high crossover straps. By 1936 *Vogue* was showing some of the first very short boots, not even reaching the ankle. When the Second World War broke out, ankle-high boots had become an established part of the fashion scene, in bright and pastel colours, for walking and smart outdoor wear – but not for indoors.

Sandals were very popular throughout the decade, for beachwear, for parties and, gradually, for smart wear with daytime clothes. As a result, courts with cutaway toes were introduced in 1936: they were an immediate success, and slingback versions followed swiftly. By 1939 everyone seemed to be wearing these shoes, even on the city streets. *Vogue* was scandalized and published candid shots of such 'lack of good taste' taken in New York and London, maintaining that it was both unhygienic and bad for feet to wear these shoes outside the house or the office. But it was wartime necessity and not public opinion which ended the fashion; such frivolous shoes were not produced during war years.

New manufacturers and retailers were mentioned in shoe editorials. New machinery made production quicker and cheaper, and new materials began to be used. Chevron-woven linen and silk mixture, very hardwearing fabric, became fashionable for sports shoes during the early part of the decade. It was later used, as was pure linen and other fabrics and mixes, for smarter shoes too.

They had all the advantages of low price, flexibility, comfort and long life, could be dyed in bright tones, pastels and even printed. Suede was perhaps the most widely used leather, also capella, a brushed calf hide which was very soft. Suede was often reinforced with leather details and walling, a strip of leather sewn around the base of the shoe to protect the toe from scuffing. Crepe de chine and satin were popular for evening, particularly in mid-decade; velvet too, before 1932. However, kid and suede, so much more practical and hardwearing, progressively took over. Lizardskin was used for sportswear, and antelope and 'serpent' skin remained chic throughout the period.

There was considerable development of non-leather soles, particularly for sports shoes. In 1934 some of the first rubber-soled shoes appeared, built onto linen uppers: thus began the modern tennis shoe. Wooden and cork soles began to appear on *Vogue*'s pages after 1937, the cork at this time usually covered with cloth or leather: in the next decade the texture of the cork was to become a fashion note in its own right.

Shoe colours seem rather calm after the previous decade. In 1930 black and brown predominated for everyday, brown and white for sports shoes, perhaps ruby velvet for evening; 1934 brought a brief reappearance of coloured legs, stockings in solid tones analogous to the shoes. Pastels came into fashion in 1935 and lasted through 1936, when bright coloured kid, particularly raspberry and green, appeared. Dark grey, dark blue, rust, all became standard colours. Black was popular for all shoes, piped in gold or silver for evening, in patent leather appliquéd onto suede, or in plain crepe de chine.

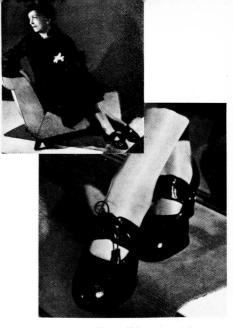

Lady Mendl, well known arbiter of fashion, considered comfort a major criterion in choosing fashionable shoes, and her attitude became general in the thirties. Here she wears rounded shoes giving toes maximum movement. F V 1935 Horst. *Pierre Viliseck*

Navy calf walking shoes with unusual shaped bar, and simplest silver kid shoes with cutout front for evenings. B V 1932. *London Shoe Company, Lilley & Skinner*

1940

A V 1932 Bruehl-Bourges. *Jay-Thorpe, Bergdorf Goodman, Saks-Fifth Avenue, Vanity Boot Shop, Bergdorf Goodman, Bonwit Teller*

'The maximum of chic per foot: let your shoes and gown agree in colour!' High heels, almond toes, for early thirties summer shoes. Blue satin sandals, *this page left*, worn with a McCutcheon crepe roma, next to perfectly plain pumps (increasingly popular) with mulberry-and-white McCutcheon crepe.

Cleverly handled straps, *left*, create an unusual sandal in yellow crepe and silver kid, worn with McCutcheon printed crepe as are the shoes, *second left*, in pink suede. A Wanamaker silk dress is worn with the dyeable suede sandals *second from right*, and green crepe sandals with T-straps end the line.

The thirties brought health-consciousness into fashion. All active sports were smart, each having its own and specially designed clothing and shoes. Naturally the feet inside the shoes (and the legs) had to be fit; the legs, *this page*, were photographed for a feature on getting the body into shape: the shoes flat, comfortable, the ideal thirties summer sandals. Espadrilles with ghillie lacing, *below*, worn by the Marquise de Montesquiou-Fezensac for sailing.

FV 1934 Steichen

FV 1932

BV 1936 Kitrosser

Society at play: *above* Eunice, Jack and
Patricia Kennedy pose for American *Vogue*
in 1938. Jack, in holiday spirit, wears
espadrilles, bermuda shorts. His sisters wear
tennis shoes, rolled down socks, playsuits.
The bicycling craze in Paris, *above*, for two:
the Princesse Jean-Louis de Faucigny-
Lucinge in flat sandals, Jacques Février in
brogues. 'The most professional tennis
shoes' – buckskin sneakers – and perfect
fringed golfing shoes, *near and far right*.

AV 1933 Remie Lohse. *Saks Fifth Avenue* AV 1933 Lohse. *Fortnum & Mason*

33

AV 1938 Be
Schiaparelli
Laird Schobe

A V 1936 Bolin. *Henri Bendel, Edouard*

A V 1936 Bolin. *The Tailored Woman/Bergdorf Goodman*

A V 1936 Bolin. *Saks-Fifth Avenue*

A V 1936 Bolin. *Nancy Haggerty, Delman*

Opposite, Benito in a surrealist mood depicts the newest, platform-soled sandals, so ornate 'you're apt absent-mindedly to put them away in your jewel-box'. This wartime fashion shape reappeared in the seventies. 'For a dinner dress of dark blue organza add, one night, red, unexpectedly frivolous red patent sandals, the next night put on the floridly printed linen sandals,' *this page top left*. 'Let's say you have a bright printed costume,' *top right*, 'go in for this dark rose linen pump, or wide open black patent leather sandal; suppose your white linen suit flaunts a red blouse,' *below left*, 'wear it to Belmont with a white and blue shoe, high cut and toe-revealing, or to a tennis match with a sandal of leather strips'. 'For a floating dress of mauve chiffron,' *below right* 'give it new vitality with either a fuchsia or green satin sandal, low or high cut.'

Vogue

'Ladies, look at these eight pairs of absurd feet. Could any of these be yours? We said to our candid cameraman, "Go out on the street, Fifth Avenue or any street, and get some snaps of open-toed and open-heeled shoes in action." There was no need to burlesque them; the naked truth was bad enough . . . We publish these pictures to show . . . beyond the power of words . . . how women look on the sidewalks of New York in toe-less, back-less, high-heeled slippers . . . These skeletonized shoes were never

Protests! Open toes and open heels are not for city streets

designed for walking; they were presented for evening and for very formal afternoon occasions. Footwear for the street should have a certain integrity, a suitability for its function . . . *Vogue* still maintains that women who really have taste and a knowledge of the fitness of things do not wear them for walking the city streets.' Thus *Vogue*, in all editions July 1939, launched an all-out attack on the wearing of 'unsuitable' shoes in the street, as opposed to closed shoes. Wartime leather shortages and utility restrictions on shoe styles won *Vogue* a temporary victory. The war over, open-heeled and open-toed shoes swept into fashion; *Vogue* silently retreated under the assault.

A V 1940 Pierre Roy. *Perugia/Saks-Fifth Aven*

Panchromatic pantoufle, *opposite*, in surreal seascape by Pierre Roy. The boot is made from crocheted, multicoloured string, on a wedge sole covered with kid. This type of upper (here depicted as other-worldly and strange) did in fact become commonplace during the war, particularly in Europe, when leather supplies were short.

'Banded boots: their swaggering stripes, their high cut, smooth as a hose, put one in mind of Renaissance gallants. Kid evening boots, wide straps band your foot horizontally – one severe enough for day, one frivolously ruffled like a garter. Schiaparelli showed these four in Paris. The carpet-slipper comfort of this embroidered bootie would complement a housecoat.'

B V 1939 Jean Pagès. *Perugia*

1940

The Second World War severed the ties of fashion between the United States, Britain and the rest of Europe. All communication became difficult, the passage of raw materials and finished goods almost impossible: convoys were vulnerable and their use naturally restricted to vital stores. Working conditions in France and Britain were difficult too, labour and supplies short due to the war effort. France was the most severely affected. She had been dependent on imported leather supplies before the war to meet her own needs and her large export commitments to the rest of Europe and the States. Thus leather shoes could not be bought (even with 'tickets') in wartime France; any shoes available were wooden-soled, with uppers of string or scraps of fabric. French *Vogue* was given the choice of collaboration or closure and chose to shut down in May 1940.

In Britain supplies were short too, British *Vogue* advocated 'make do and mend' for old clothes and shoes, and promoted Utility clothes and shoes: the Utility mark was given to styles which combined good (and standardized) design with very modest fabric requirements. Women were wearing holes in the soles of their pre-war shoes (for even re-soling was an extravagance). Comfort and long wear were British *Vogue*'s criteria; that provided by Utility shoes, very different from its American counterpart, was the comfort of high-laced masculine shoes in black, browns, chestnuts, with heavy, even wooden soles.

When leather was used, it was often brogued or pebbled and very rigid. At the beginning of the war a number of crocodile, snake and lizard shoes came onto the market, the last stocks of these valuable leathers, which were obviously not suitable for boots for the Forces. *Vogue* encouraged women to brighten their shoes with coloured piping (ribbon was not rationed) and laces, and to find alternatives to the stockings which soon became scarce. Leg make-up was unattractive, messy and cold; socks were the only viable alternative. Ankle socks were, moreover, cheap to make: *Vogue* published patterns for home knitters, even suggesting that they should unravel old jumpers and use the yarn.

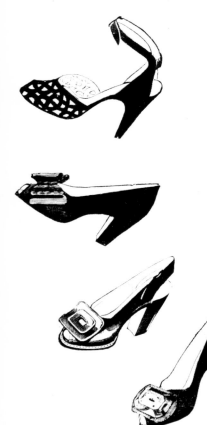

Ankle straps, bows and peep-toes on high-heeled day and cocktail shoes. AV 1944. *Delman*

The USA had much greater national resources of raw materials than Britain or France, and her clothing industry was thus less immediately affected by the War. After the States entered the war in 1942 there were more restrictions, but coupons were not issued: American clothes and especially nylon stockings were the envy of Europe.

The shape of shoes changed a great deal over the decade. In 1940 heavy wedge shoes and platforms were still high fashion, and French, British and American *Vogues* had just begun to show a new lighter shoe with a slim high heel and squared toes. This trend continued in the States: bright light shoes were the fashion note of 1941, and the whole decade is full of them. New light and very flexible shoes were developed, uppers made of fabric and Lastex combinations for ultrasmooth fit. Bright canvas and heavy cottons were used for uppers too, and layers of coloured kid to build up a 'piled' heel. Walking shoes were the only sombre note, low chunky heels and wedges with laced and buckled uppers.

The excitement of the liberation of France in 1945, the end of the war and the return of the warriors did not bring an end to shortages and rationing: it was not until 1948 that life began to return to normal. French *Vogue*, which reappeared joyfully with a special edition in 1945, gradually returned to its pre-war size and frequency. British *Vogue* began again to show lively shoes and clothes. The New Look came on 12 February 1947, heralding the return of the waist, and of the feminine curves which were no longer bundled into airforce blue or landgirls' overalls.

French and English shoe designers quickly picked up the threads left loose in 1939. By 1947, when leather deliveries began to pick up speed and volume, European women were demanding new styles to fit their new freedom and clothes shapes. Light, revealing shoes appeared very swiftly, often giving little support to the foot – as frivolous as the New Look which was no respecter of fabric shortages. The whole look was a tremendous success in both Europe and the United States, and suddenly all the old links of fashion were reforged.

The new shapes of 1947 and 1948 were more rounded, a perfectly natural answer from the designers to the general craving for a softer life after the hardships of the war. Sports shoe fashions returned; the latest ski and après-ski boots and clothes became a regular autumn preoccupation in all *Vogue*'s editions. Toes became less chiselled, wedge soles very light in their new thin form, even made of rubber for flexibility. Strapped shoes came back into fashion, straps with rounded ends and little buttons (which had been rationed). Ankle straps were an important new note, indeed all kinds of sandals and peep-toe shoes were popular and referred to by *Vogue* as 'the new post-war tradition'. Fabrics were those strangers from the thirties: velvet, kid, coloured leathers, bright satin, and 'bronze', a burnished leather.

'Silk on its last legs': soon stockings became rarities. Shoes are masculine, business-like. B V 1941 Cecil Beaton

'Cloth shoe, froth shoe': feminine shoes again, in shantung. A V 1948 Rutledge. *Frank Bros.*

1950

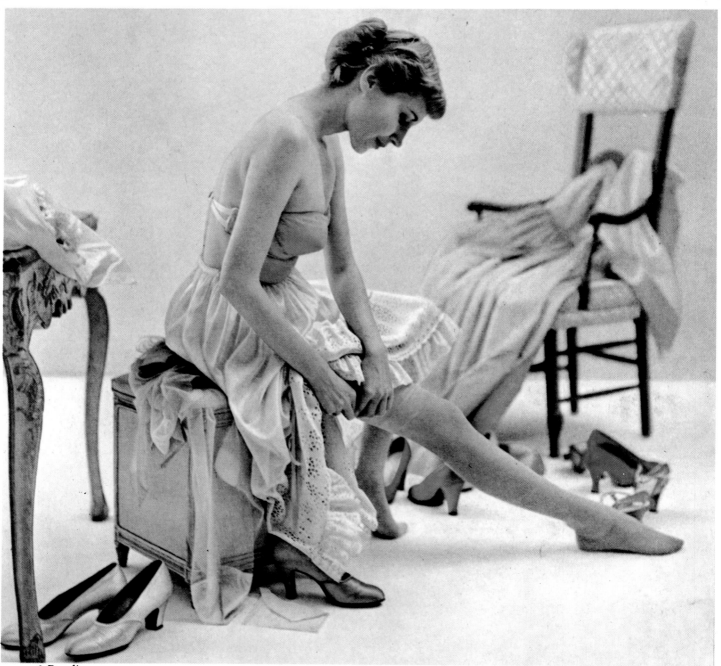

AV 1948 Rawlings

Stockings, like all clothing, were in extremely short supply in Britain and France during the war. British *Vogue* published this American picture of American merchandise, *opposite*, in 1941 when there were no more stocks of British stockings to promote. Limited numbers of these lilac, chalky-rose and apple-green stockings were available from Harrods, Fortnum & Mason and Marshall & Snelgrove, but by 1942 most women were bare-legged all summer, in socks for winter. Nylon stockings appeared in America in the early forties: in Europe during the war, nylons appared only as gifts. Fine, easy to wash, knitted to mould the leg, they immediately became the most popular type of stocking. Shoes, too, are lighter, more feminine: the heavy wedge of the late thirties and early forties, *opposite*, has disappeared in favour of court shoes with finer heels, lighter, higher sandals, shiny leathers.

B V 1942 Lee Miller. *Left to right: Lilley & Skinner, Brevitt, Joyce, Pinet, Delman, Lotus*

BV 1941 Lee Miller. *Clockwise from shoe in hand: Abbott, Lillywhites (2), Lotus (2)*

BV 1942 Lee Miller

BV 1943 Lee Miller. *Brevitt*

Shoes at war: 'Prolong your single accessory', ran the caption for these shoes, *opposite*. Some of the last pre-Utility shoes, they are nevertheless designed for long wear, practicality. Several have wedge soles (another example of these *right*), popular for their simplicity in construction and comfort in wear, four are of calf, all have contrast piping, a popular wartime method of brightening plain shoes; one is crocodile-skin, one suede pigskin. *This page, above:* 'Shoe shine for your precious calf shoes, and your still more precious patent, last relics of unrepeatable stocks from France. Don't leave them to the "boots"; shine them yourself using the right polish: proper cleaning prolongs the life of leather – and that is now an affair of national importance. Your shoes can last the duration if you pay a good price for them, keep them well polished.' Shoes were not the only problem. Stockings were scarce, and by 1942 women were wearing short socks like these, *above right*. Some were using last stocks of yarn, or unpicked jumpers, to hand-knit stockings like the openwork pair, *below right*; this pattern was available from *Vogue* on request. The shoes have 'rocker-last' wooden soles which were hard wearing and used rubber (another precious commodity) only for heel and toe tips.

Eric

1947 Arik Nepo
1948 Eric

Clothes and shoes for
foreign travel: active and
passive sports like skiing
and sunbathing once
again, after the War,
became fashion
preoccupations. *Opposite*
are the latest ski boots of
1947, *far left*, worn with
black and chartreuse
ski-pants and a chartreuse
waterproof. Après-ski,
too, has its own special
boots, in soft suede with
crepe soles and over-
lapping flaps with buckles
at the ankles. For the sun,
right, American *Vogue*
suggested that readers
should 'keep skin fair',
wear an all-over make-up
specially formulated to
prevent tanning and
burning of skin – even
that exposed between the
straps of these flat,
comfortable beach shoes.

v 1948 Horst. *Saks-Fifth Avenue*

A V 1948 Bouché. *Urbanite/Altman*

BV 1948 John Ward. *Russell & Bromley, Bally*

Christian Dior's New Look of 1947 voiced a whole
new mood in women's clothing. Just as fabric
shortages had reduced skirt widths and sleeve
lengths to a minimum, leather shortages had meant
that only the most practical closed shoes were made.
Bouché's drawing, *opposite*, shows the new soft, full
line in a Larry Aldrich dress of navy-blue rayon
crepe with rayon taffeta petticoat, the new open
shoes with skeletal straps. *This page above* are two
strappy evening sandals, one with a little wedge sole,
narrower now than in wartime, suede ankle straps
and high heel. The other has three broad scalloped
straps, also of suede, which form the vamp.
Newest of all: 'Florentine' gathered suede boot,
right, softest shape of softest leather, snugly drawn
in around the ankle and perched on a high, narrow
heel. Ankle boots were very fashionable in the late
forties, elasticated, buckled, on wedge soles, and
many of the shapes were copied in the late seventies.

BV 1948 John Ward. *Holmes*

A V 1949 Blume
Newton Elkin

Newly bright leathers – blues, greens, yellows, reds – to match or contrast with everything. Colour and finish of shoes was the most important factor now: *right* are two of calfskin, burnished, cut low over the instep, the other of rust leather with T-strap.

Softer shape for a softer life: the shoes of 1949 were almond-toed, cut to mould to the foot, on high tapering heels. Ostrich opera pump, *opposite*: 'Oh, she's NOT a contortionist, really. We gave her a leg up by borrowing it from a window display mannequin to arrange this otherwise "impossible interview" – a *tête-à-pied* between blond tones.'

1950

Patent evening shoe
with suede drape
over the instep,
echoes the waistline
of the dress. BV 1959
Willy Ronis. *Carvil*

Tess D'Erlanger in
the new mood of
the fifties: 'pretty,
not too sophisticated
– and simple and
tidy and young'.
BV 1958 Vernier

The post-war resurgence of ultra-femininity in women's clothes continued into the fifties. The early part of the decade was a time of sharp cut: *Vogue* described Fath's spring collection in 1954 as 'almost self-conscious in its detail, the precise silhouette is found throughout, slim-fitting as a glove'. The shape of clothes did change quite radically, from Hourglass to Tent, to H-line, to A-line, to Sack, to Trapeze, as the seasons passed. The changes were not gradual: like the shapes, they were clean-cut, collection severed from collection, sometimes even designer from designer. The look was one of serious chic, a studied look with a hint of archness, for the new angular shapes accentuated the body's curves, revealed it with clever cut and decolleté. Shoes fulfilled a similar function for the feet; their shape changed in unison with clothes, but changes were less sudden and obvious. Heels narrowed, then widened, rounded toes became points, became squared again. Beautiful 'naturally' clad legs and arched slender feet are a mark of the decade. Ultra-sheer and sheer stretch stockings arrived to flatter the legs, some even had decorative seams (seams slimmed the legs) or tiny embroidered flowers at the ankle, but none hid the shape of the leg as the bulky knit and rib tights of the next decade were to do.

Shoes were arched, sophisticated, erotic, cut away to reveal the maximum of the foot, perched on narrow, delicate heels. Heels were high in 1950, but by 1954 there were a great variety of heights for different occasions and times of day. The infamous (it destroyed every floor it touched) stiletto arrived; it had a heel so narrow that it appeared pointed. By the second half of the decade lower, squat heels were becoming popular, as were 'flatties' with no heel and a flimsy sole, largely for wear in the house with trousers. The 'spool' heel, so called because of its resemblance to a thread spool, was very popular in 1952, and although its large diameter went out of fashion, the circular heel remained fashionable. In a lower and less dangerous form, the fine stiletto heel was still worn in 1960 – although *Vogue* was preoccupied by newer developments.

The separated front and back shoes of the late forties continued, and ankle-strapped versions appeared. The court shoe was very low cut, at the sides and top of the foot, and almond-toed. Gradually this shape became more pointed, and by 1958 Dior cut the point off the shoe completely to produce the new and influential 'wedge' shape. Continuing into the sixties, this shape was increasingly used for flatter shoes. Some court shoes had tiny straps, others ghillie lacing or little tabs, to emphasize the slenderest part of the foot just above the toes, where the courts had been cut away. Large bows, too, were used on simple pumps in 1957, made of chiffon, grosgrain ribbon or satin ribbon. In 1955 Givenchy introduced a new-shaped court – cut straight across the instep – and called it the 'opera pump'. It had a lower heel, wider too, and the shape was important for several years. Sandals and mules, in particular, were popular. The back of the foot had been a centre of interest in 1950, when courts with appliquéd heels, diamanté embossed heels and quilted leather heels had been shown. By 1951 the heel of the foot itself was on display, in mules and sling-back sandals designed for smart wear and not solely the house or the beach. T-strapped courts were very popular from 1958, strapped from a very low front. The alternatives to the various heights of narrow heel were the lower, broader-heeled pumps, or really flat shoes with 'egg-point' toes, in firm leathers, both of which were popular with the younger set. This type of shoe, tomboyish by comparison with its contemporaries, was wearable with denim jeans and playclothes. Its advent heralded the end of the ultra-feminine era in clothes and shoes in favour of a rather flexible look in fabric, shape and function.

The sweeping changes from season to season were the death throes of Haute Couture as it lost ground to 'ready-to-wear'. In London, for example, graduates of the newly established Royal College of Art fashion design course were not moving into Couture but into the new boutique market, and demand was increasingly for the avant-garde, not for 'good' clothes and shoes. Mary Quant's first boutique opened in 1956, in the King's Road, catering for teenagers who wanted their own style, not just a watered-down version of what their mothers or sisters wore. Almost immediately, her designs went on sale in America. In British *Vogue* itself, in early 1958, Tess D'Erlanger, fashion assistant, modelled clothes and shoes captioned as a 'not too sophisticated' look.

The colour and fabric of the shoe were of secondary importance at the beginning of the decade: the shape was everything. Fabric tended to be a smooth leather or soft suede in black or brown. For evening, colours were brighter and the fabric satin. Ribbon details on daytime wear had become brighter too, broad grosgrain and satin ribbon for laces, rouleaux too (laced shoes were particularly important in 1952). The craze for all things Oriental, in the fashion world of 1954, brought Turkish slippers, in deep hues and embroidered with gold beads, onto the market. The craze died, but the shoe colours and fabrics of 1955 show how extensive the influence of the mood had been: watered silk courts appeared for evening wear, as did mules, printed leather day and evening shoes, coloured soles in the new Neolite. Printed linen inners made a brief appearance, and lizard, punched leather, bronzed leather, all came and went. The decade finished with a crop of 'eggshell' finish leather shoes, in oyster, beige, white and cream: this treatment of leather remained tremendously popular at the beginning of the sixties. The Italian no-heel court of 1959 was fun, with its metal 'sole-support', dazzling in red silk and hopelessly impractical.

New gloved arch, spool heel for a softer tread. BV 1952 Herbert Matter. *Ferragamo*

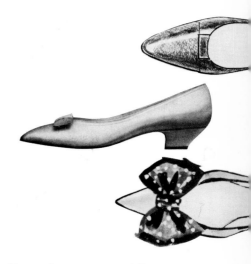

Egg-point toe. BV 1958 Bouret. *Bally of Switzerland*

The young look: party-happy pump. BV 1958 Vernier. *London Shoe Company*

Ottoman pump with spotted bow. BV 1957 Bouret. *Bally of Switzerland*

1960

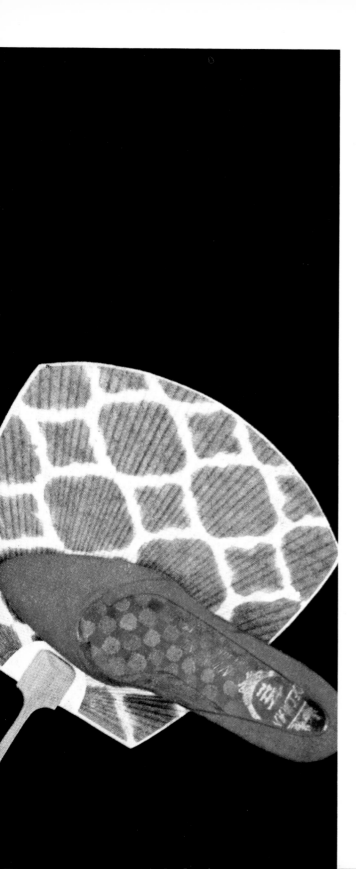

B V 1954 Cecil Beaton. *Dolcis*

New fabrics of the fifties in American and British *Vogues*.
'The view of the new southern shoes shown [*opposite*] is
a rare one: once a woman steps inside them the print's gone –
but not forgotten. The printed shoe-lining principle is the
same one that printed coat-linings thrive on.' The two
Delman shoes are lined with printed silk, the other two with
printed calf; the outers are of suede and leather. Oriental-
look evening outfit, *above*: metallic threaded hopsack
trousers, Goya-pink shantung shirt, gold-embroidered
violet suede pumps with leather soles, all very Arabian
Nights.

A V 1956 Rutledge. *Clockwise from bottom left: De Liso Debs,
Delman, Mademoiselle, Delman*

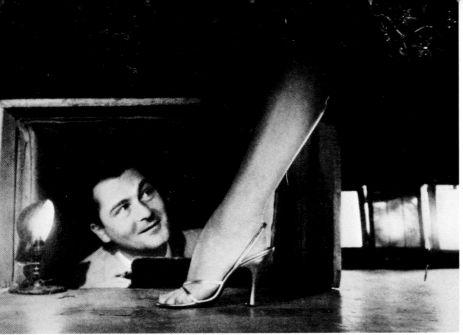

FV 1953 Robert Randall. *Jordan*
FV 1954 Rubin. *Perugia*

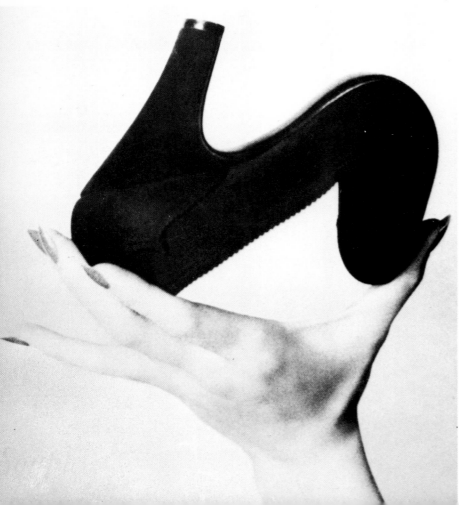

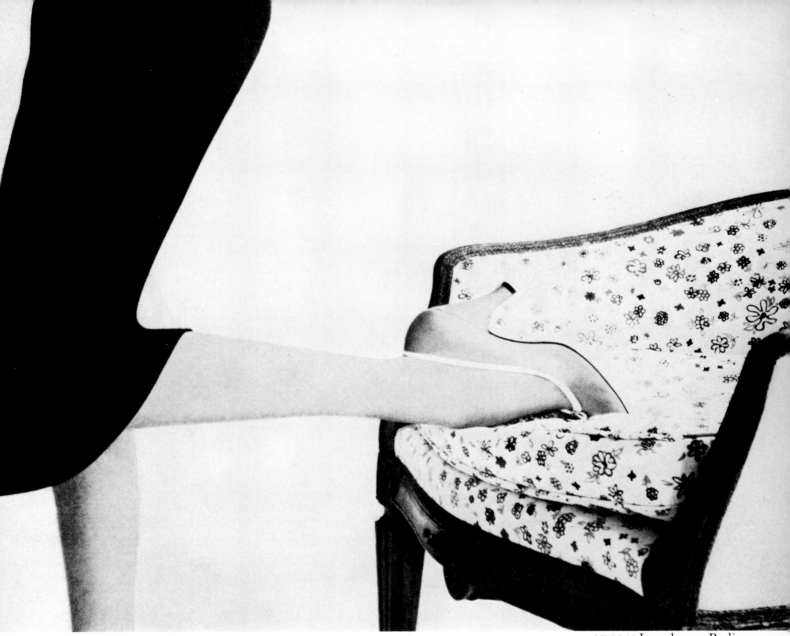

A V 1955 Leombruno-Bodi

The new moods in elegance for the feet. *Opposite below*, the ultimate in sensuality: Perugia's court shoe, as 'supple as a glove, completely constructed without rigid shank, able to follow the movement of every muscle without losing its shape'. For shoes in the footlights the mood is arch, confident, extrovert, like this shoe, *opposite above*, of gold and green kid, set on a high, narrow heel; playwright Georges Vitaly watches intently. The simple court shoe, *above*, is in a calmer, more casual daytime mood, as slim and fitting as the wearer's skirt. Made from pastel calf trimmed with white, the shoe rests on a chair upholstered in printed leather, an attractive craze in the fifties when extended to shoes, too.

57

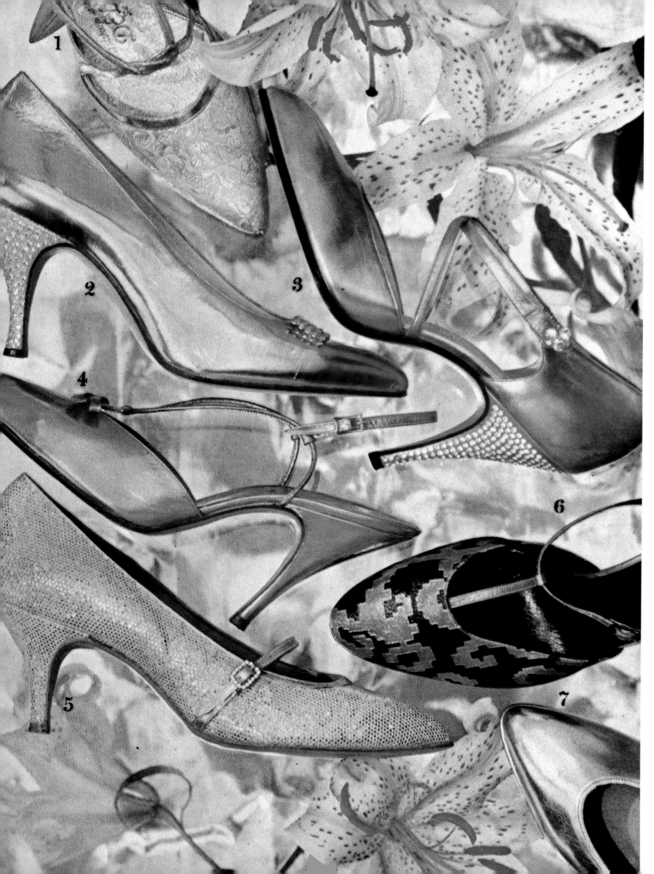

The stiletto in all its heights and finishes, for day and evening. Gold and silver shoes return to fashion with a vengeance, *this page*: all these are of kid or brocade and highly burnished; the toe shape varies from almond to pointed, treatment from simple to finely strapped, with rhinestone buckles, heels, buttons. Lizard shoes, as fresh as paint, *opposite*, in cardinal red with ankle strap, delphinium blue with chiselled point, laurel green. Delicate, sophisticated, these shoes mark the height of the stiletto's popularity and the zenith of the very feminine look.

BV 1958 Caradog Williams. *Delman (1), Lotus (2), Pancaldi (3), Saxone (4), Lilley & Skinner (5), Russell & Bromley (6), Dolcis (7)*

BV 1958 Caradog Williams. *Holmes, Turner, I. Miller*

Alternatives to the
stiletto: no heel at
all! The shoe,
opposite, was
handmade in Italy
for Delmanette,
using a metal
extension of the sole
as support.
Needless to say, the
idea did not catch
on.

A very practical
alternative, how-
ever, *this page*: a
look especially
created for the
fashionable young
whose voices were
becoming ever
louder. The shoe is
pointed, low, in
satin and broderie
anglaise, the heel
comfortable but
still with the smart
sharp look.

1960

'Clothes that are all dash and zing are a way of life. Anyhow. Any age. Temperament and a fair set of bones call the fashion shots, not the age filled in on your Blue Cross Card.' (American *Vogue*, 1962.)

During the sixties the last vestiges of curviness disappeared. Toes became more chiselled, heels less and less waisted: by the end of the decade they were often completely straight. In clothes too, the movement was towards straight lines and few curves: the look 'clear cut and crisp', said British *Vogue* in 1965, 'propelled by positive contrasts of textures and colour'. Courrèges' spring collection in 1964 had set the pace: it was space-age, geometric, banded with straight lines of colour to smooth out natural roundness; the shoes were decorated with cut-out patterns, and white boots were also shown. Fashion now underwent the change that had been heralded in the fifties, whereby the 'trend' was splintered into many different fractions. Ready-to-wear collection themes filtered through fast to boutiques, and fashions changed with equal speed. 'Throwaway' ideas abounded, and paper dresses came and went. Various 'looks' were available at any one time, in shoes as much as clothes. Mary Quant's early sixties 'little girl' look immediately became very popular. There were blouses underneath little tunic dresses in black, brown and bright, childlike flatty shoes over thick-ribbed or patterned tights which enhanced the ever-increasing expanse of leg on view. 'The audacity of fashion is in the legs,' said French *Vogue* in 1964; 'it's obvious because they're all we can see!' Skirts got shorter and shorter: the miniskirt arrived mid-decade and remained news for some years. Thus appeared boots, filling the gap left by the shrinking skirt: some boots reached the thigh, some stayed below the knee, at first loose with a front seam, later tight to the leg.

The return of the long boot was assured after Courrèges' crop of shiny

Courrèges launches the geometric, space-age look. B V 1964 Norman Eales. *Bally of Switzerland*

Clean-cut, solid-heeled shoes in shinies. B V 1966 Barney Wan. *Dior above, St Laurent below*

Throw-back to the twenties: punched black and white kid shoe *left* and bone leather shoe with black toe cap and Louis heel *right*. B V 1965. Terence Donovan. *Rayne*

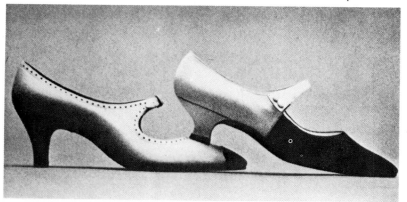

British *Men in Vogue* 1966
Michael Cooper

Anita Pallenberg with
Brian Jones of the
Rolling Stones, he in
'co-respondent' black and
white shoes which she
chose, Anita in the
fashionably low-heeled,
ankle-strapped sandals
which could be worn at
any time of day or
evening. Both these
sandals and the shoes
opposite have the childlike look which was
fashionable throughout
the early and mid-sixties.
Flattish, with little
squared heels, in lizard
(*opposite left*), eggshell
leather (*opposite right*),
patent, wet-look, they
looked good with short
skirts and thick
patterned tights.

A V 1967 Penn. *Juliane*.

B V 1964 Cowan
Russell & Bromle

white boots in his spring 1964 collection; for more than a decade after this event, boots were hot fashion news. Sports aside, boots had not been in fashion for fifty years (but had for many years been the characteristic garb of prostitutes in some cities). As the sixties progressed fashion boots became tighter to the leg. At first they were made of plain leather or plastic, but later versions used treated leathers, textiles, appliquéd leathers. Perhaps the most popular was the 'wet look' boot, extremely shiny and soft (unlike patent). The process was used on fabric and leather to produce a fitting and comfortable high boot.

After 1963 the heel widened, but remained narrower at the base than the top until 1968. As the geometric look went out of fashion and a softer shape reappeared with peasant and ethnic clothes and prints, shoe shapes became even more solid, heels broad and squarer; in some cases the base of the heel was wider than the top. Soles thickened too, often to quarter-inch thickness, and were covered with suede or leather.

The squared almond toe, whether combined with stiletto heels or with the newer 'stacked' leather heels, was *the* shape at the outset of the decade. Some shoes were strapped high up on the instep, others were ornamented with flat little bows on punched leather. By 1962 the shoe was quite rigid-looking, often in patent, with broader heel and sharply squared toe. *Vogue* in 1963 and 1964 was full of closed or sling-back little pump shoes on a low blocked heel, with the geometric cut-outs which are so evocative of the sixties. White lace stockings completed the 'children's party' look.

After 1967 the low-heeled pump began to disappear in favour of a higher and strappier shoe with a thick sole. Oriental-look sandals with jewelled encrustations appeared, and the exotic mood spread to other shoes in gold or silver, with embossed and jewelled heels. Flat lace-ups, cut low over the instep, or sandals, were good with everything as alternatives to the ubiquitous boot; all now had a much more solid look than had been usual earlier in the sixties.

Black, in patent and wet-look leather as well as calf, was very important. The soft colours of the early years – olive, bronze, soft natural wood colours – gave way to bright shiny green, navy, white, scarlet – and aubergine, the colour of the late sixties and early seventies. By 1971, an aubergine pair of shoes was to be the staple of every fashionable wardrobe. Paisley fabric-covered shoes were popular in 1963, but in general plain, pearlized or shiny colours were the vogue. Gold sandals and evening shoes were popular, as were shiny or contrasting buckles for day shoes.

Shiny vinyl and wet-look treated leather or man-made fabric were the newest shoe textiles in the sixties: as leather prices rocketed and supply could not keep up with demand, added impetus was given to research into alternatives, with results reaching the market quickly.

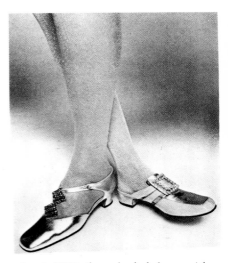

Louis XIV silver shaded shoes with courtly jewels and matching stockings. BV 1967. Montgomery. *Luini*

Essential fashion item now: the boot, here worn by Alexandra Stewart. FV 1967 Henry Clarke. *François Villon*

1970

v 1965 Art Kane.
lianelli

In complete
contrast to the
clean-cut, often
space-age look of
most clothes:
Oriental shoes and
clothes came into
fashion mid-
decade. This
blue-and-silver
kidskin sandal on
hand-painted
platform was a
shape which became
mainstream fashion
in the late sixties
and early seventies.
The chopine *right* is
an ancient Oriental
shape, designed to
keep the feet dry in
wet and dirty
streets. Purely a
'fun' shoe in this
context, it is of
wood and kidskin,
worn with equally
patterned leotard.

A V 1965 Art Kane.
Evins/I. Miller

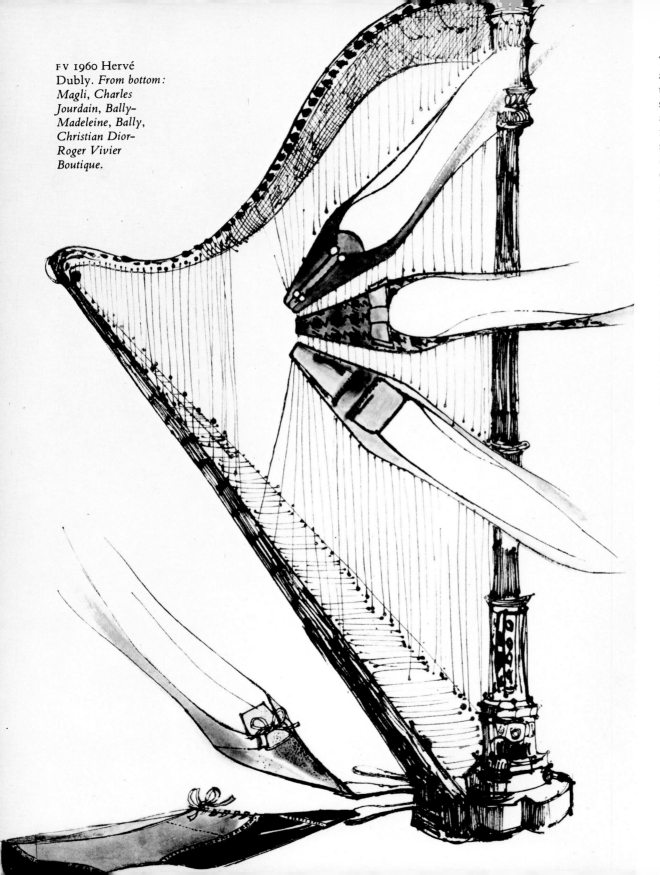

FV 1960 Hervé
Dubly. *From bottom:
Magli, Charles
Jourdain, Bally-
Madeleine, Bally,
Christian Dior-
Roger Vivier
Boutique.*

The changing heel
and toe shapes of
the early sixties. The
sharp, pointy heel
and toe of the
mid-fifties were
still around in 1960,
below left two
examples of the
shape updated with
the trademarks of
1960: exotic wood
colours, punched
holes, two-tone
leather and patent,
and bow. The
paisley mule,
opposite above right,
is a lower version of
the fifties stiletto,
but new and
important is the use
of multicoloured
fabric uppers. The
new heel is the
more solid one
opposite below,
becoming straighter
and wider every
season; the new toe
is the pen-nib
shape, top left,
widening
throughout the
sixties like the heel.
And with all these
shoes, fine, pale
leg-coloured
stockings, here from
Charnos, Wolsey
and Berkshire.

BV 1963 Mau
Pascal. *Bally
Boutique.*

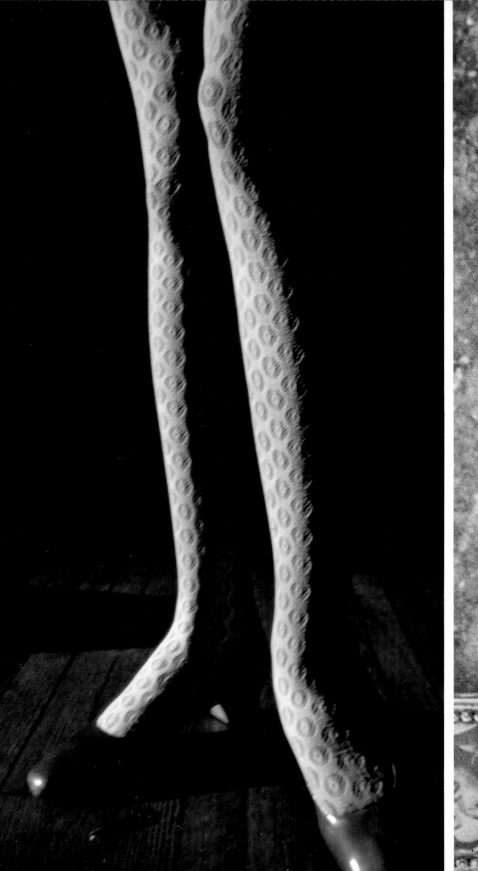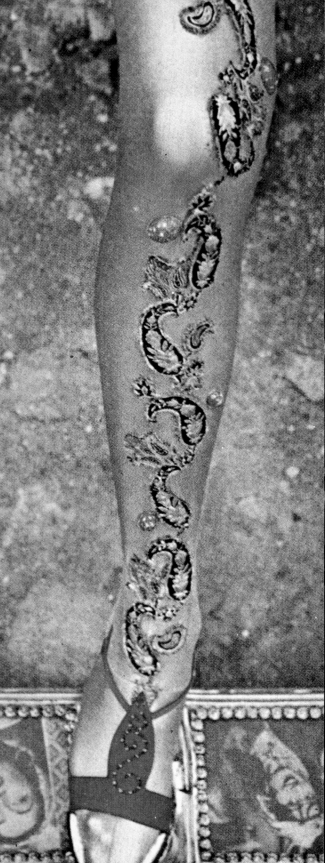

1968 Art Kane.
entina

1965 Art Kane.
Miller

Shortest skirts, mid-sixties, give lots of scope for painting the canvas of leg and foot. And tights quite naturally become the smartest leg-gear, 'the waist's the limb-it: all-time high for stockings now'. *Opposite left*, the top street fashion, simplest-shaped pumps on low, walking heel, with tights in harmony, their circular cut-outs echoing the rounded shoe shape. Variations on the theme, in Turkish mood, *opposite right*, shoes and stockings richly embellished with precious stones, stockings of stretch nylon lamé, sandals of Indian silk. Further East still, *this page*, cobra sandal, of the snake's skin dipped in gilt, with rubies for eyes, crimson soles, coiled around a leopard-spotted leg.

A V 1965 Art Kane.
Fleming-Joffe/Lord & Taylor

v 1968 Jeanloup
eff. *Charles*
urdan

Black and white,
matt and shiny:
strong contrasts in
shoes. *Opposite*, the
ankle-strapped,
separated front shoe
which was popular
throughout the late
sixties and into the
seventies. Here in
black patent with
white cutouts, it was
a very versatile,
practical style. *On
this page*, elegant,
white, buckled shoe
in patent (patent
and wet-look were
very popular at the
end of the sixties)
with chiselled toe,
narrow silhouette
contrasting strongly
with the thick,
chunky stocking.

A V 1968 Art Kane.
*Divina/Altman
Young Colony*

BV 1969 Guy Bourdin. *Ravel*

BV 1966 Peter Rand. *Bally of Switzerland (top), Kurt Geiger*

Courrèges' dramatic spring collection in 1964 shocked and delighted the fashion world. From this beginning stemmed a geometric, space-age mood in fashion. There were no soft or rounded shapes. Instead hard, sharp outlines, hard bright colours mixed with white-toned pastels, hard fabrics like patent for shoes, stiff shiny fabrics for clothes, even 'chain-mail' mesh, plastic shapes ringed together. The Courrèges look of 1964, *opposite*, almost threatening in its severity: the famous boot makes its entrée in shiny kid, below the knee, loose-fitting. Bright version of these boots, *this page left*, worn with bright space-y outfit. The pastels in patent and suede, *above*, their cutouts in keeping with the look: sharp, hard outlines.

BV 1964 Helmut Newton. *Giusti/Russell & Bromle*

1970

One of the most popular shapes of the seventies: the clog. BV 1971 Barry Lategan. *The Chelsea Cobbler*

Roller skating à la mode. BV 1975 Toscani. *The Chelsea Cobbler*

The shoes of the seventies were as lively and adventurous as the women who wore them. *Joie de vivre* was the mood: as the decade progressed the ideal woman was not only happy and relaxed, but fit and glowing with health too. 'Be yourself in fashion,' said *Vogue* in 1974, 'and you can live nine lives at once.'

Yet at the outset of the decade platform shoes and boots (already daringly high) had risen to alarming levels, provoking fears from the medical profession that the spines of the fashionable would be irrevocably damaged. Wedge soles, too, became extremely high. The word of the early seventies was 'psychedelic', meaning in contemporary usage no more than a whirl of colour. Psychedelic boots were painted with other-worldly designs, appliquéd with suede 'fruit' and 'flowers', patchworked with bright mixes and clashes of colour. After 1975 shoes lost their high platforms, wedge-soled shoes became lower and lower, the elegant high heel returned in its lightest and strappiest form, flat and heeled brogues moved into smart day-time fashion. By the end of the decade a sea-change had taken place in the shape of shoes. Still bright and lively, they were a different breed, light and delicate, revealing the foot and moulding to it, rather than simply decorating it.

The thickening of the sole which began at the end of the sixties continued into the seventies, reaching its zenith in mid-decade when the fashionable were wearing soles 2 inches thick (and even higher ones were produced). Heels thus reached a total 5 inches high in some cases. Wedge soles gradually took over from platforms and became high too; they remained fashionable throughout the decade and by 1979 were popular in a low, sculpted form, rather like that of a clog. Heels and soles were now often made of textured fabrics, cork or rope in addition to crepe rubber and leather-covered plastics or wood. The stumbling walk of the early seventies disappeared as a new strain of lighter shoes began to appear: flatter leather sandals and lace-ups, wedge-soled or traditional flat espadrilles, elegant high-heeled court shoes and evening sandals.

The early seventies were very creative years in shoe design. New fabrics and finishes were experimented with, new shapes appeared, new shops too: shops selling own-brand high fashion shoes swiftly made up after the collections at selected factories, often in Spain. Lace-up shoes and boots were the most popular shapes in the first two years of the decade, in suede, punched leather and in canvas, one of the most used fabrics of the decade. Leg-laced shoes were the continuation of the laced boot: espadrilles and sandals, even court shoes often had laces mid-decade. The separate-front ankle strap shoe was another important early shape, on a platform or wedge

Boots, boots, boots, the essential for every wardrobe through the seventies, almost to 1980. BV 1971 David Bailey. *Left to right: Meucci/ Russell & Bromley (2), Charles Jourdan, The Chelsea Cobbler*

sole, later with a fine heel and thin sole. One of the best-selling shapes was the mule: at first wedged, with an upper of canvas, leather, printed fabric, tapestry, patchwork, vinyl, suede, later equally popular on a cone or high slender heel, in 1978–79. But best-selling style of all was the boot. Knee-length or higher still until mid-decade, it was followed by the ankle boot from 1976 until the early eighties. Much shoe design fervour was channelled into the styling of boots at the beginning of the seventies, with beautiful and fantastic results: silver platform boots, rainbow-painted boots, brightly coloured canvas boots. After the demise of the platform, colours and designs were less fanciful: short boots had a forties flavour, often made in suede with little turnbacks. The fashion for jogging brought its own shoes, satin-covered canvas or leather in bright colours to match tracksuits. Roller skating became a method of transport as well as a sport and acquired all-in-one boots-on-wheels, or separate bright shoes and skates.

Colours and fabrics for shoes were myriad in the early seventies. Texture was all-important: shiny in 'wet-look', raised surfaces in tapestry, embroidery, patchwork, appliqué, rough surface in canvas, printed hessian and natural linen, matt in suede. Smoother plastics and leathers were used too, but chiefly in painted, patchworked or silvered form. In the second half of the decade, however, these smooth leathers became of prime importance, as did suede. Colours were plain, often deep tones; 'shinies' were popular too, gold and silver for evening shoes and sandals and even for cowboy boots, clear Perspex, glitter and shiny beads embroidered onto leather. Leather substitutes like Corform, marketed mid-decade, received much publicity, but leather remained top favourite and came back strongly at the end of the decade. Synthetics were, however, increasingly used for soles, being invisible in wear and more resilient than leather.

And so into the eighties in a burst of colour. High, strappy sandals (with the bare minimum of coverage), high mules, running shoes, moccasins all appeared in shocking pinks and fuchsias, lime green, emerald, sapphire, every startling colour. As lively, in fact, as the girl wearing them, who made swimming, running, workouts in the gym and a sensible eating plan part of her life. All very reminiscent of a similar mood in the thirties when active sports became *comme il faut*, with special fashion shoes for each sport. As American *Vogue* pointed out: 'there's the realization – well established by now – that good looks and good health are inseparable'.

Flattest pumps, gilded. BV 1980 Alan Randall. *Midas*

1980

The mood of the seventies was lively, adventurous, colourful. New fabrics for uppers, new soles too: Suede and canvas were two of the most popular. *This page*, green and rose suede curvy sandal, ending in flowers at the ankle (these cutout shapes, as here or appliquéd, were an early seventies craze). The soft, comfortable crepe sole is new too, fashionably high for 1971, lower later. Canvas espadrilles *opposite*, ever-fashionable shape, laced up the leg for the seventies (lots of other shoes were too), on a low wedge rope sole rather than the traditional flat shape. Rubber tips on the sole gave grip.

BV 1971 Lester Bookbinder. *Manolo Blahnik for Zapata*

IV 1973 Rizzo. *Vergottini (left),*
Alberti (right)

BV 1971 Tessa Traeger. *Andrea Pfister*

'What's a nice boot doing in a fabric like this?' ran the caption for these boots, *opposite*. Colours and fabrics for shoes and boots were myriad in the early seventies, experimentation by young designers produced boots like these, of towelling patches in paintbox colours, cotton Madras 'patch' (both fabrics from Liberty of London), and lilac canvas starred with navy blue on a cork wedge sole. The platform was important throughout the seventies, at first thickening, up to two inches thick under the toes, later slimming down again to quarter-inch thickness. Spangles and sparkles, satin fabrics, diamanté all abounded. These T-strap wedge sandals, *this page*, with red glitter plastic flames, green satin uppers were high fashion for evening (and perhaps even day).

BV 1971 Tessa Traeger. *Chelsea Cobb*

AV 1971 Penn.
Left to right:
Charles Jourdan,
Herbert Levine,
Charles Jourdan

The non-stop leg: leotard and tights, with tiny miniskirt and all eyes on the expanse of patterned and striped leg, and on the bright new footgear. Three proportions of boot, *left*, embroidered purple (single most influential colour of the decade) velvet, ankle-high purple suede, below-the-knee red suede lacing over fur inner. Newest shoes for wear with mini suits: lace-ups with small chunky heels, in very shiny punched 'wet-look', and in suede, with very neat, tailored appearance. With all these go a huge range of thick and thin knit tights (which have long since taken over from stockings as most worn legwear), socks in bright colours. Flowers on sixties stockings and tights have now ceded to hearts and checks for the seventies.

AV 1971 Pen
Left to right:
Julianelli, Ch
Jourdan,
Mademoiselle
Charles Jourd

Platform soles and solid, squared heels: the ever-thickening sole looks hopelessly impractical and uncomfortable, but was worn for walking, even motor-biking, *opposite*, in one of its most radical forms. Dark suede, as here, was very popular during the first half of the decade; the shoes *on this page* are of white matt-finish mock leather, strapped around the ankle, a softer version of the platform.

1971 David Bailey. *Mr Freedom*

The brightest, zaniest young shoes of 1971, *opposite*, the most exciting year in shoe design since the twenties. Hand-painted with rainbows, clouds, stars and moon, they were fresh, 'way-out', bright, clear in both colour and design. Shoes in Pop art, *this page*, are platform-soled, strappy.

FV 1971 Helmut Newton. *Charles Jourdan*

BV 1975 Lategan. *Biba*

Feet in fashion: sandals frame the foot now, a foot which has to look healthy, fit, well cared for. Scholl's foot refresher, *opposite*, for a night of dancing in these high sandals with fine, knotted straps. 'Wallpaper' fabric shoes on high wedge sole, a very popular shape, with pedicured toenails painted to match, *above*. The most open, glamorous sandals, *this page right*, white and scarlet, reserved for feet which, like these, are treated with loving care and lots of moisturizer.

BV 1975 Lategan. *Midas*

BV 1977 Lothar Schmid.
Manolo Blahnik/Zapata

BV 1974 Graham Hughes. *Saint–Laurent Rive Gauche*

Shoes as accessories after the fact. Innocent victims, *this page*, at the mercy of a malicious lift: high patent and gold–chain sandals, with sheerest stockings. The aggressors, *opposite*, the most elegant violence in bronze lizardskin, sharply shaped heels, two broad straps over the foot.

AV 1977 Von Wangenheim *Geoffrey Beene*

1977 Eric Boman. *Charles Jourdan*

IV 1979 Fabrizio Ferri. *Casadei*

Heels at their height in the seventies.
Opposite, heel like a ferrule, slim steel shaft on
ice-blue leather shoe, tied around the ankle.
Equally high, elegant, but less vicious are the
cone-shaped heels on the suede court shoes
above. The cone was an important shape in the
late seventies, both high, as here, and in a
lower form on a rounded little pump. *Right*,
a more traditionally shaped heel, but very tall,
tilting these stunning legs forward, in their
fine, seamed black stockings. The upper is
delicately cutaway: the most popular sandal
shape in the late seventies.

FV 1978 Laurence Sackman. *Christian Dior*

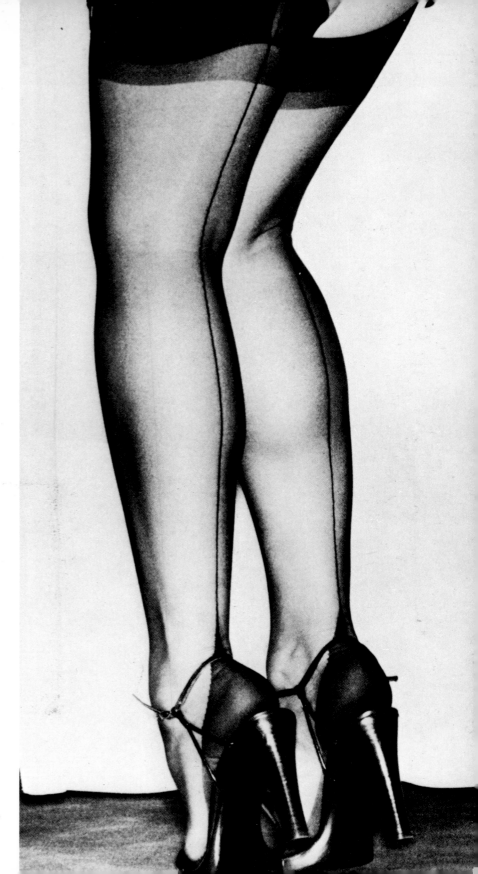

G V 1980 Michel
Momy. *Andrea
Pfister*

The shoe-like boot
of 1979, very bright,
very tall on its
elegant, curved, but
slender, heel. These
ankle boots had a
very forties feel
about them, both
in shape and
leather, suede was
particularly
popular for these in
both decades. *On
this page* the light,
strappy sandal of
1980, with fine,
rather vicious heel.

B V 1979 Albert
Watson. *Charles
Jourdan*

Healthy fashion: bright satin sports shoes to race around the clock, matching shorts. BV 1977 Willie Christie. *Kickers*